POWERFl
WHILE
CONQUERING
PRINCIPALITIES

Recognizing the Powers of God

Thank you Mrs. Terri for all of your support.

Love Loraine Hammell

POWERFUL FAITH WHILE CONQUERING PRINCIPALITIES

Recognizing the Powers of God

LORAINE TRAMMELL

EXPECTED END

ENTERTAINMENT

Atlanta, GA

DEDICATION

I dedicate this book to others dealing with any [MHD] Mental Health Disorder, such as depression, schizophrenia, bipolar and all other disorders. Whatever obstacle or principalities may occur in your life, never give up and never give in. Trust in the powers of God to guide you and keep you. You must have faith that all things are possible through Christ Jesus.

CONTENTS

ACKNOWLEDGEMENTS

I give God all the glory, honor and praise for keeping me and directing my path. Although this journey of trial and error is tough, I will remain focused and I'm yet holding onto my faith and achieving my destiny.

Special thanks to my pastor, Rev. Jerry Black, for the tutelage of inspiring words of encouragement that have truly made an empowering impact on my spiritual growth and allowed me to keep pressing my way through every obstacle.

Special thanks to Mr. Chuck Brown for taking on this project and providing excellent quality service. I would also like to thank my industry goddaughter, Michelle Lovett, for all of her support and thank you for all that you do. As I continue my spiritual growth towards the next level, I know that all things are possible through Christ. I am a woman of God walking with a passion and a purpose.

CHAPTER 1

GOD'S MIRACLES WHILE CONQUERING EVIL FORCES

The world has encountered many demonic forces. People are facing personal attacks throughout the nation. My first born encountered a serious brutal attack in January 2015. The Athens Police Department of Tennessee was involved in a violent act of combative force with my son. This was devasting news for my family to receive.

I can remember receiving the call from my son's father as if it were yesterday. I was in shock. I was on an emotional rollercoaster with my thoughts all over the place. Yet, I had to keep it together mentally because I had to get on the road and travel alone, even without knowing all the details of what happened, what to think or what was going to happen.

This demonic attack occurred during the midnight hour, according to the police report. The date reported was January 25, 2015. I received the phone call around 8 a.m. that morning. My son was admitted into the ICU. My heart dropped, at least that's the feeling that I had. My heart was extremely heavy, and I was emotional as I wanted to know everything, especially my son's condition.

It was the longest three hours of my life. I could barely concentrate on the road as I drove because of my tears and my mind racing about my son. Within three hours of receiving the call, I arrived in Tennessee. The doctors informed me that if my son had lain in the grass 20 more minutes where the police found him asleep, he would have died due to the cold weather. The medical report states that all my son muscles had collapsed due to the freezing temperature.

I began to question everything I heard and read in the police report. Police said my son attacked six officers. Where did he gain all this strength to hurt and attack six officers, especially since the doctors informed me that my son was laying in the cold for hours, minutes away from freezing to death because of his body temperature. So, I still can't comprehend what could have caused these officers to use such brutal force on my son. The doctors stated that he had no strength due to his muscles collapsing. I began my own investigation. It was not adding up to me and I needed answers. The doctor's reports and the police reports weren't matching.

My son was diagnosed with chronic depression and schizophrenia and takes medication for his condition. The police officers were not aware of this young man's medical condition. However, this does not excuse the officers' excessive force. The doctors reported they found too much of the prescribed depression medication in my son's system. Improperly taking his medication caused my son to react in an abnormal manner, which led him to wander outside of his apartment, leaving his door unlocked and went for a walk in the wee hours of the night. He lost track of his state of mind and tried to go back home. Apparently, he wandered off, not far from where he lived, in a nice quiet area near an elderly facility. That's where two police officers found him asleep in the grass, in the freezing cold temperature. They called for backup and four more officers arrived on the scene.

Ephesians 1:20-21: *"Which he wrought in Christ, when he raised him from the dead, and set him at his own right hand in the heavenly places. Far above all principality, and power, and might, and dominion, and every name that is named, not only in this world, but also in that which is to come."*

LORAINE TRAMMELLL

CHAPTER 2

KEPT BY THE POWER OF GOD

My son remained in ICU for five days fighting for his life. The cold weather contributed to him being there. But the brutal attack by six officers also was a major factor in his condition. The time of the attack was never mentioned in the police report. According to their report, it said the time of incident was unknown.

The Tennessee police officers stated in the report that upon arrival on the scene, my son was found asleep in the grass. He was unconscious with no shirt on and shaking. Frost covered his eyelids and his hair, which means he was lying there for some time. I'm extremely emotional as I tell this portion of one of life's horrific principalities. Yet, the process had to take place for me to empower others that may experience attacks from evil forces of this world.

Psalm 121:5,7-8 – 5) *The Lord is thy keeper: the Lord is thy shade upon thy right hand. 7)The Lord shall preserve thee from all evil: he shall preserve thy soul. 8) The Lord shall preserve thy going out and thy coming in from this time forth, and even for evermore.*

After reading the police report again, I asked myself the same question I asked before... If my son was in such a bad condition when officers arrived, why did the six officers nearly beat him to death? Police stated that my son just jumped up and began attacking them. Now as a mother, I've always taught my children to respect the authorities and their elders. My children have always been well-mannered. The police never mentioned that my son was tasered while they tried to detain him. You would think that at least one of the six officers on the scene would have recognized that something was wrong with this young man, especially seeing him in the condition he was in.

During this brutal attack, my son received a black eye, busted lip, several taser marks on his neck area and face, a huge gash in his head, and a gash behind his ear. His wrists were cut because of the handcuffs being applied so tightly that they were cutting into his veins. He lost an enormous amount of blood. His elbows, shoulders and lower back were scarred from being dragged. His body had several other bruises as well.

The officers stated that they had to detain him because he was attacking them. My son should not have been treated like an animal from this type of attack. It was vicious and horrific. I often have to take a break and allow God to minister to me because every time I think about what my son went through, I get angry. But I thank God that my son is still alive. He survived that beating. If my son did lash out at officers, I could now imagine how startled he must have been. However, the Holy Spirit showed me that my son merely was fighting for his life. My son was not in his right state of mind due to the amount of medication that the doctors found in his system. They believe he took his medication improperly, as if he was trying to overdose. However, that was not the case. Later, my son told me he was not trying to overdose. He had forgotten that he took his medicine earlier. His memory is very short now and he constantly repeat the same thing.

The six officers should never have beaten that 21-year-old unarmed male. He was lying there dying with no strength, according to the doctor's report. Six officers on one black male. They should have at least recognized, through their professional training, that something was wrong with a person lying in the cold with no shirt or coat on. The police officers abused their authority towards detaining my son. To me, this treatment appeared to be race driven. Cruelty, bodily harm and mental suffering was added to his already complicated situation. Now, he must live with that experience and those memories for the rest of his life. This savagery, barbaric, unjustifiable and inhumane treatment caused by professional officers of the law has caused life-long pain. They were sworn to protect and serve the people.

Ephesians 6:12 says, *"For our struggle is not against flesh and blood, but against the rulers, against the authorities, against the powers of this dark world and against the spiritual forces of evil in the Heavenly realms."*

CHAPTER 3

RECOVERING FROM AN ATTACK OF THE ENEMY

The six police officers involved in my son's attack should not be employed on anyone's police force. They are dangers to society and not protectors of the people. Law enforcement is placed in position and designed to help people, not hurt them. They need more training on how to handle abnormal situations. The police report states that my son awakened in a combative force and that the family stated that he was violent. That is a lie. No one in the family made that statement. I believe he was tased several times prior to rising and that caused him to rise striking the officers. That does not make it right. However, the officers should have known not to provoke someone who was already disoriented. The young man was unarmed!

The doctors stated that my son had been unconscious so long in the cold that it caused his muscles to collapse. Their report states that excessive taser usage and muscles collapsing caused his CK ENZINE count to be extremely high and almost cost him his life. But God had another plan! The police department wanted to file charges against my son.

I began my own investigation. As a mother, none of the charges made sense to me. Because the attack was so brutal, I felt this was about racism and every officer truly should have been dismissed from the force! I placed on my spiritual antenna and went into meditation, calling on the Holy Spirit to guide me. The next thing I knew, a family member on his father side was a member of the NAACP in Tennessee. That family member arranged a meeting with the chief of police. By the time I was released from that meeting, God had already worked it out. All three charges that were supposed to go against my son were dropped.

While lying in the hospital bed, and with me staying with

my son, he remained conscious long enough to give his life back to God.

Yes Lord! All we did during his recovery was listen to the word of the gospel, including sermons on CDs from my church. I was guided by the Holy Spirit to take a few CDs and the cd player to minister to both of our souls during his time of healing, trial and tribulation. Hearing a familiar word of God from our pastor, Rev. J.D. Black, helped him tremendously. He was receptive to the word of God and asked me if he could re-dedicate his life to Christ? If only you can imagine how I felt knowing that God's anointing took over the atmosphere. I am beyond thankful that I was able to witness the supernatural wellbeing of God! Every nurse and doctor that entered that room had something positive to say about the spiritual anointing in there. As they came and left, they complimented us and said, "Thank you for playing that CD." Some even asked for prayer.

I was called to pray for others when I needed prayer myself just to make it through the next day. Won't God do it! God allowed my son to receive the best of care during his recovery, maintained my strength and allowed my son to regain his strength. I remained in Tennessee at the hospital until he was released. Even though I felt emotionally drained, I stayed my course in the Lord. I kept my faith strong. I know without any doubt that God is a keeper!

JOHN 3:16 – *"FOR God so loved the world that he gave his only begotten Son that whosoever believeth in him should not perish, but have everlasting life."*

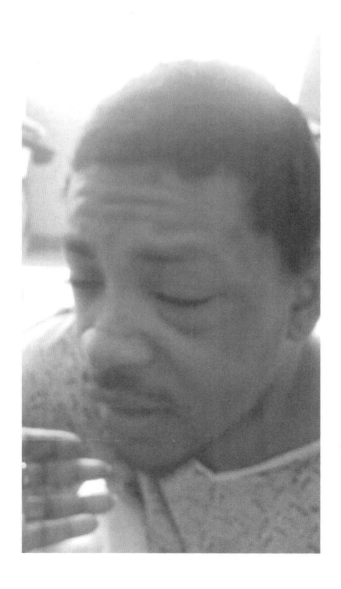

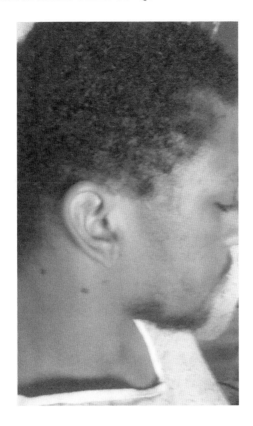

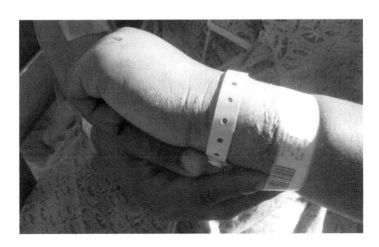

CHAPTER 4

CONQUERING PRINICIPALITIES

Other Narratives not authorized for print? None
Narratives this user authorized to print.

Narrative by: Patrol Officer Regus Nichols (APES02) Division: Patrol APD

Date & Time 01/25/2015 11:52	Narrative Description	Entered by Patrol Officer Regus Nichols (APES02)	Status View	Reviewed by	Last Edit Date 01/25/2015

ON 01/25/14 I OFFICER NICHOLS RESPONDED TO A CALL WITH OFFICER AMBER WALKER AT LIFE CARE CENTER ON FRYE ST IN REFERENCE TO A MALE SUBJECT LAYING ON THE GRASS AREA NEAR THE BUSINESS WHO APPEARED TO BE UNCONSCIOUS. PRIOR TO MY ARRIVAL OFFICER WALKER HAD ALREADY ARRIVED AND REQUESTED E.M.S. TO RESPOND TO THAT LOCATION. UPON MY ARRIVAL I MADE CONTACT WITH OFFICER WALKER AND THE SUBJECT WAS STILL LAYING IN THE GRASS. SHE STATED THAT SHE CHECKED FOR A PULSE AND ATTEMPTED SEVERAL TIMES TO GET HIM TO RESPOND TO HER. SHE STATED THAT HE WAS SHAKING AND APPEARED TO HAVE AN ELEVATED HEART RATE. HE WAS LYING ON THE GROUND WITH NO SHIRT AND APPEARED TO HAVE BEEN THERE A LONG PERIOD OF TIME DUE TO FROST ON HIS EYES AND IN HIS HAIR. I THEN ATTEMPTED TO WAKE THE SUBJECT WITH NO RESPONSE. I ADVISED OFFICER WALKER THAT WE WOULD HAVE TO AWAIT E.M.S. TO EVALUATE HIM FURTHER. AT THIS POINT THE SUBJECT JUMPED STRAIT UP AND TURNED TOWARD US AND STARTED YELLING. HE CAME TOWARDS US IN AN AGGRESSIVE MANNER THROWING PUNCHES IN OUR DIRECTION. HE IMMEDIATELY TURNED HIS ASSAULT TOWARDS ME CONTINUING TO THROW PUNCHES. I ATTEMPTED TO BACK AWAY FROM THE SUBJECT SEVERAL TIMES AS HE CONTINUED TO LUNGE FORWARD ATTACKING ME. AT THIS TIME I WAS STUCK WITH CLOSED FIST TO THE SIDE OF THE FACE AND A PHYSICAL STRUGGLE TOOK PLACE. I ATTEMPTED TO DEFEND MYSELF AND OFFICER WALKER WHO WAS ALSO BESIDE ME. AT ONE POINT I WAS ABLE TO TAKE THE SUBJECT TO THE GROUND AS HE WAS STILL STRIKING ME WITH HIS FISTS. OFFICER WALKER WAS THEN ABLE TO ADMINISTER A BURST OF HER DEPARTMENT ISSUED O.C. CHEMICAL WEAPON TO HIS FACIAL AREA. THE SPRAY DID SLOW HIS ATTACK FOR A FEW SECONDS. THE SUBJECT THEN BEGAN ROLLING ON GROUND AS I HAD BACK OFF REALIZING THAT I WAS BLEEDING FROM MY FACE AND TRYING TO GAIN MY COMPOSURE. I THEN ATTEMPTED AGAIN TO TAKE THE SUBJECT INTO CUSTODY AND RESTRAIN HIM IN HAND CUFFS. ANOTHER BRIEF STRUGGLE ENSUED AT WHICH TIME E.M.S. HAD PULLED ONTO THE SCENE. AT THIS TIME BACK UP OFFICER WALKER AND MYSELF WERE ABLE TO PLACE THE SUBJECT INTO CUSTODY. AT THIS TIME BACK UP OFFICERS SPO JACKIE HOLMES AND OFFICER ERIC LONG ARRIVED ON SCENE AS WELL AS SEVERAL SHERIFF'S DEPARTMENT UNITS. THE BACK UP OFFICERS THEN ASSISTED E.M.S. IN LOADING THE SUBJECT INTO AN AMBULANCE AND TRANSPORTED HIM TO STARR REGIONAL EMERGENCY ROOM DUE TO HIS CONDITION AND INJURIES. SPO JACKIE HOLMES THEN SPOKE TO MYSELF AND OFFICER WALKER ABOUT OUR INJURIES WE RECEIVED DURING THE STRUGGLE AND STATED THAT WE ALSO NEEDED TO RESPOND TO STARR REGIONAL FOR TREATMENT. WHILE AT THE E.R. OFFICER WALKER WAS TREATED FOR INJURIES TO HER KNEE AND SHOULDER. I WAS SEEN FOR INJURIES TO MY HEAD AND HAND. I WAS GIVEN A COUPLE STITCHES FOR A LACERATION TO MY LIP AND HAND WAS PLACED IN A BRACE FOR A STRAIN TO MY THUMB. IT WAS DETERMINED THAT THE SUBJECT WAS DAVID A SIMPSON WHO RESIDES AT MCMINN VILLA BESIDE LIFE CARE. HIS FAMILY STATED THAT HE HAS A HISTORY OF MENTAL ILLNESS AND HAD RECENTLY BECAME VIOLENT. I ADVISED SUPERVISORS THAT I WOULD BE SEEKING CHARGES ON THE SUSPECT FOR THE ASSAULT TO MYSELF AS WELL AS THE ASSAULT TO OFFICER WALKER AND RESISTING ARREST. MR. SIMPSON REMAINED AT THE HOSPITAL AND WE WERE ADVISED BY STAFF THAT HE WAS GOING TO BE ADMITTED TO THE INTENSIVE CARE UNIT AND WOULD REMAIN HOSPITALIZED OVER NIGHT. STAFF AT E.R. WAS GIVEN AN INTENT TO ARREST FORM FOR MR. SIMPSON. AFTER BEING RELEASED FROM THE E.R. I RESPONDED TO THE STATION TO COMPLETE NECESSARY PAPER WORK AND ISSUE THE SAID WARRANTS ON MR. SIMPSON.

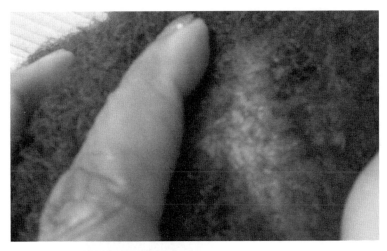

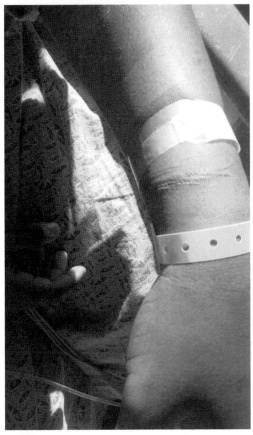

LORAINE TRAMMELLL

CHAPTER 5

EITHER YOU TRUST GOD OR YOU DON'T

December 5, I received a phone call around 3:30 a.m. from Mr. P, the new in-house chaperone at the facility I would leave my son for watch care. As I answered the phone, I felt something was wrong, especially at that hour. And it was. Mr. P stated that my son was missing. With my heart pounding, I asked him what did he mean "missing"? I frantically pleaded with him to tell me what happened. In times of disturbing news, you can't allow your mind to become overwhelmed because it's easy for your mind to conclude the worst. I had no idea what could have occurred. Mr. P told that the police had been called. However, the police could not file a report because it had not been 24 hours since he went missing. The police were able to file a (BOLO) Be on Look Out report, with an explanation that this was a case with a person dealing with schizophrenia.

My son was a part of a different program four days prior to being accepted into the new program that assisted young men experiencing illnesses such as his. He was not familiar with his new surroundings, which caused him to wander off in the middle of the night. He left the doors wide open at the new location, while everyone was still asleep. That's not good at all! Once I gathered my sense after hearing the disturbing news, I began contacting all the hospitals and all the jails in Georgia. No one had a John Doe or a David, because he did not keep up with his ID. The emotions of being a parent started rising from the depth of my soul. I became extremely emotional. I could not stop crying. After hours of searching for him, I continued to pray and ask God to please step into my situation. The thought of my child was in the world just wandering with no money was excruciatingly painful. I was worried because since he was diagnosed with schizophrenia, his memory was not on point. He forgot a lot of details.

I had to completely trust God to bring us through! It was impossible for me to locate him especially when I just didn't know where to look. The state of Georgia was a huge territory. I became wearier. I could not go back to sleep. Soon, it was going to be time to get ready for church. I knew that God was amid my weariness. However, my faith was strong enough to also recognize that God was dealing with me from a new level of supernatural, divine intervention that I could not even imagine!

The sunlight was coming through the window. Yes, I was grateful to arise and see another day. Yet, the tears remained from this hold on me that I just could not seem to shake. I began my morning with another prayer and started my Sunday routine in preparation for church. I meditated and gave my problem to God... at least I thought I did. I arrived at church and participated in praise and worship. During the service, Pastor called people to the altar for prayer. As I approached the altar, my mind so heavy with the news about my son. I instantly began talking to God. I said, "I submit my all to you, my heart, my soul and my mind! I trust that you will send a divine miracle. Lord, I truly give this task to you."

When I left church, I asked God to please let me know where my son was and for him to be ok.

Because of so much corruption in the world and the dangers facing young black men, in particular at the hands of the police, that load was heavy for me to carry. I had to continue encouraging myself and trusting that God would not place any more on me than I could bare.

Midnight had arrived and there was still no news on my son's whereabouts or wellbeing. It was Monday morning, day 2 of him being missing. I had to remain strong because I was due

21

at work in a few hours. Upon my arrival, I was back to being an emotional wreck, only this time I had to inform my boss of what was going on with me and my family, just in case I had to abruptly leave. I broke down again as I began to explain to my boss, and I had to excuse myself until I could re-gain my composure. As I returned to my desk, my emotions toned down slightly, but I was still feeling so heavy with anxiety. I was breathing extremely hard, sweating, and I felt as though I were about to fall out of my chair. Instantly, the Holy Spirit took over my thoughts! I was convicted for not completely trusting in God. I was trying to remain calm at my desk, but the Holy Spirit asked me, "Do you trust in God?" I was shocked because I thought I did trust God and didn't understand why I was being asked that. Then the Holy Spirit said, "So, why are you sitting here crying yourself to anxiety? Did you not bring your heavy burdens and your impossible, to the altar just yesterday? Either you trust me completely or you don't."

What a mighty and powerful wind of the anointing rushed through my body. I straightened up and began thanking God for all my blessings. I thought about the story in the bible when Abraham was willing to sacrifice his son. I knew then that I had to be willing to also sacrifice my son. Instantly, I yielded my impossible over to the Lord. I told the Lord, "Whatever your will may be, let it be done in the mighty name of Jesus."

I wiped my tears away and began to smile. I named and decreed that my impossible was not too impossible for God to handle! I could not control the divine supernatural feeling that I was encountering. It was so comforting to me. God is so amazing! All you have to do is be a willing vessel for Christ, and he will fight your battle. God can handle the impossible when you can't see the possible. All of this occurred around 9 a.m. "I don't know how, Lord, but I truly trust you. My back is up against the wall and I have no other way out but through you."

Lunch time had arrived. I decided to devote my entire hour to Christ, through prayer, devotion and worshiping God. I felt so good about the miracle of God that my son would be located. I did not know when nor how, but I believed God was going to answer my prayer. I knew God would not allow me to suffer long without knowing where my son was or if he was safe. I continued my prayer constantly and continued to encourage myself.

When I returned from lunch, around 1:30 p.m., I received a phone call on my cell from a number that I did not recognize. I anxiously answered it in hopes that it would be my son trying to contact me. My son always remembers my number no matter what state his mind is in, especially dealing with this ugly disease called schizophrenia. His medication does not help his memory at all. Back to the phone call… clinching as I answered the call, "Hello…"

"Ma!"

"David! Son, how are you? I'm so glad you called me. Where are you?"

The excitement was overwhelming. I just began crying tears of joy, thanking God, of course! I knew that he would not talk too long to me because of the side effects of his medication. I immediately asked him if he was near or with someone. He answered and said yes. I asked him to put them on the phone.

I overheard the voice in the background as he tried giving

them the phone. They said, "Who is that and what do they want?" He told them it was his mother and that I wanted to talk to them. The lady was slightly irritated, but I began to explain my son's situation of him being on medication. The elderly lady then began to sympathize. She then began to explain to me that my son wandered into their facility, which was a homeless shelter located in Marietta, Ga. We then arranged for me to pick him up. Once I picked him up, I began asking him how he got all the way to Marietta from Atlanta. He said he walked.

During that time of the year, it was cold and a lot of heavy rain. I still often wonder how this young man survived that storm? He only had a coat with a hood attached, no gloves. My! My! My! God is such a keeper and he's still alive. Although he had to be hospitalized to get his medication back on track, all I could do was praise God even more. I realized that the Lord was transitioning my faith to a higher dimension that I could not imagine. I call this my very own supernatural gift from God!

When it looks impossible for you to handle, it's simply possible for God! Look at God! Won't He do it! I now have a new direction in life and a new perspective towards my destiny. I know for myself the magnificent powers that my Lord is capable of. God wanted me to experience this miracle to allow me the platform of sharing with others about what my God can do.

People have so many trials and tribulations in their everyday living. However, people that recognize an assignment placed upon them should be willing to share their testimony to help others endure. That is how your blessings will flow. While going through your process, it is so important that you are vigilant and recognize what God is revealing to you.

Luke 10:19 – *"Behold, I give unto you power to tread on serpents and scorpions, and over all the power of the enemy: and nothing shall by any means hurt you."*

LORAINE TRAMMELLL

CHAPTER 6

THE PROTECTION AND COVERING OF GOD

Life's obstacles were meant to kill me, but God had a master plan for my life! When you submit your soul to the Lord and are willing to allow God to use you, doors will begin to open. God will take you to a higher dimension to allow your vision, new birth and opportunity to bless others. I learned to surround myself with positive people with a vision, who are ready to move into action. I've grown to trust the process of my life's obstacles that God has placed before me. The challenges are extremely difficult at times, but I manage to press my way through it. As I reflect on the journey, I now see the progress of my spiritual growth during my own obstacles.

You can only trust mankind but so much. While attempting to build a relationship, a person must prove their loyalty towards me before they gain my trust. If you are not careful and cautious, mankind will let you down, disappoint you, hurt your inner being, and crush all your feelings. But God will never leave you nor forsake you.

Be aware of the revelation that God is trying to show you. Let me tell you a little about my situation in dealing with a program called The Recovery Program, funded by the state of Georgia. While experiencing an encounter with my son, I realized that the state of Georgia does not have many programs or facilities to accommodate young men ages 19-28 who are battling mental health illnesses. I experienced a bad encounter with The Recovery Program where my son went for help with his schizophrenia.

It's imperative to stay involved with your loved one if he or she is a part of any type of program or facility that has authorization to administer medication for the illness or disorder. The Recovery Program suggested my son be placed in a special recovery program that could provide the type of assistance he required. It was a voluntary admission program, so my son had to make the decision to enter. However, the program also needed my permission because I was his caregiver and parent. I encouraged my son to enter the program. I thought it couldn't hurt him and would be a great source of information and resources to help him since it was an establishment program with a professional staff. My son agreed. This was the worse decision that I've encountered while dealing with this mental health disorder!

I learned that my son's condition escalated from imaginations and unusual thoughts to rebellious behavior and overall uncharacteristically bad conduct. He stopped trusting me and no longer wanted me around for my visits. He didn't want to go on our usual rides together and didn't want to communicate with me at all. Everything that was normal for us quickly changed.

This behavior knocked me off my feet because of the close relationship and love that I have with all my children. Each one of my children has their own special relationship with me that they can count on. Because of my son's behavior, I decided to do my own investigation. As a mother, I knew something was wrong! I'm always in tune with my loved ones' wellbeing.

I began appearing at the program without consulting with staff. Normally, I'd contact the staff beforehand to arrange visits. I would make sure that my son would not be in class or in a counseling session. Then I would confirm that he would be available for me when I visited. I switched up my routine. I stopped all the formalities and did my own motherly drive by visits!

I had already established a relationship with all the counselors, doctors, instructors and directors before my son entered the program, so the staff already knew that I was a concerned and loving parent. This allowed me access to enter as I pleased. After all, this was a volunteer program. I learned to observe every move of every employee, including their body language. I had to put on my private eye antenna.

I thought the program would help my son gain a better awareness of himself. But shortly after monitoring his behavior, I did not notice any improvement. As a parent, I was hoping and praying for positive results, improved behavior and a better self-image. I began asking questions with my son's assigned nurse. I learned that his medication had been switched without my knowledge or permission. Our agreement before the program started was for me to be informed of any and all changes concerning my son. All hell was about to break loose. I became angry and was on the verge of losing it. But I calmed myself enough to handle the facility professionally. I placed on my parental guard, my attorney guard and my armor of God! After my threat to sue this facility, I was able to remove him from the facility without any further incidents. For a while, I worried that because the program had all my son's personal information, they could sabotage him. But I had God on my side.

So many families left their loved ones in the facility without checking on them, as I witnessed during all my visits. Do not leave your loved one in the hands of the government established programs without scheduling visits on a regular basis and occasionally making surprise visits.

There are very few facilities that help people dealing with mental disorders. Someone had to be strong and bold enough to take a stand to be an advocate for those exhibiting unusual behaviors because of mental disorders that affect the entire families. The government has their own assigned doctors, nurses, counselors and therapists to label you or your loved one according to their diagnoses and prescribe medications needed. Therefore, you must know and believe in a higher source of power. Mine is called Jesus. If you do not carry the title of being a doctor, you are going to need some source of help. Yes, medications are needed, however, but you need to stay involved and monitor the prescribed dosage and observe the behavior and the conduct of your loved one, especially after each new medication is prescribed. Do your own research. You can easily use Google to find information on just about everything. And remember that communication is your best weapon to help you help them. If their character is off, step in and say something. You have that right.

This type of situation can be overwhelming at times. Yes, I have even questioned God about my son's situation. Why him? Well, guess what? Why not your son? God can do what he wants, whenever he wants. But know the situation has been ordained by God to allow you to follow through with the process. I now open my mindset to allow God to direct my footsteps. You must remain faithful, stand strong and press your way towards your purpose and your destiny in Christ. Even though your situation exists, deal with it! Until God releases you from your assigned task, He will see you through it and tremendously increase your strength. Do not give up on your loves one!

Ezekiel 22:14 says, *"Can thine heart endure, or can thine hands be strong, in the days that I shall deal with thee? I the LORD have spoken it, and will do it."*

CHAPTER 7

THE #7 (SEVEN)

THE #7 (SEVEN)

The #7 in the spiritual realm, represents COMPLETION! Victorious living through Christ is the goal!

Here are SEVEN TOOLS that will help you as you assist your loved one who is experiencing a mental health illness or disorder.

1. PRAYER

Trust and believe that whatever or whomever you're praying for will receive VICTORY!

   A. Prayer is spiritual supplemental medication that I utilize for healing on my soul. I align myself to meditation and seek help from my savior, the Lord Jesus Christ. It prepares me to be in expectation of VICTORY through CHRIST!
   B. Proverbs 3:5 - *Trust in the LORD with all thine heart: and lean not unto thine own understanding.*

2. MEDITATION

Be still. Find a peaceful place to dwell and allow yourself to hear from God and invite Him into your life to direct your path!

   A. In my preparation of meditation, I allowed myself to go on a spiritual fast, meaning eating very little and a healthy meal, such as a salad, for three days. I allowed myself to have my meal at the same time during the three-day FASTING period. You can also set your own schedule due to any medical issues. However, you must remain the course, stay dedicated, and allow the breakthrough to occur on God's appointed time!

B. Proverbs - 3:6 *In all thy ways acknowledge him, and he shall direct thy paths.*

3. BE A WILLING VESSEL TO BE USED BY GOD

Recognize your assignment through Christ and show accountability to make things happen. Once you've accepted this commitment, just watch God change things for your good!!

A. One day, during my time of separation from my husband, my children were missing their dad and wanted to hear from him or see him. I placed on my armor of God and told my children that we were going on a two-day fast over the weekend to allow me to accommodate and monitor their eating schedule. I explained to them what to expect out of the Prayer Fast and I also explained the sacrifice it would take for God to move on their behalf and cause them to see and hear from their father! We complied and fulfilled our goal. God answered the prayer request during that week. The children received a phone call from their dad! They were happy and that gave them a new reason to believe that prayer does work!

B. Proverbs 3:13 - *Happy is the man that findeth wisdom, and the man that getteth understanding.*

4. VISUAL

Guard your ministry, guard your character and guard your surroundings of associates/associations and then anticipate a divine calmness within your atmosphere!

A. Even inside the church you have to guard yourself. I've served on a couple projects within the church and people tried to sabotage each mission by being out of order during planning. I'm not condemning Christians. I'm merely speaking on behalf of what I've encountered. I had to stay vigilant and remain my course in a divine manner.

B. 1 Peter 5:8 - *Be sober, be vigilant; because your adversary the devil, as a roaring lion, walketh about, seeking whom he may devour.*

5. MAKE WISE DECISIONS

Always think before you react in public, as well as behind closed doors! God sits high and looks low with all POWER in his hands!

A. We all have made mistakes. But we should learn from our mistakes and change our pattern of thinking. To every wrong or bad decision that we have made, there was a consequence to deal with. God will allow you a second chance to correct yourself!

B. 1 Peter 5:10 - *But the God of all grace, who hath called us unto his eternal glory by Christ Jesus, after that ye have suffered a while, make you perfect, stablish, strengthen, settle you.*

6. RESEARCH ALL RESOURCES AVAILABLE TO UTILIZE DURING YOUR PROCESS

Study to show yourself approved, prepare to take ACTION and keep your FAITH!

A. Your research should consist of medically approved diagnoses. However, don't rely on just one doctor's opinion. Also, do your own investigation of the cause of your loved one diagnosis. Research all resources within the territory of the cause! Prayer works, but you need to follow doctor's instructions. You need a double portion Professional Help and Prayer!

B. 2 Timothy 2:15 - *Study to shew thyself approved unto God, a workman that needeth not to be ashamed, rightly dividing the word of truth.*

7. KNOW YOUR BLOODTYPE

This will help you and your loved one towards living healthier by eating according to your blood type. And Exercise!

A. A close friend once told me about how POWERFUL the blood of Jesus Christ is. As I looked toward the sky, I thought, "How profound!" WOW, the blood does so many things. Running a blood test can tell what's going on in the human body and the blood of Jesus already speaks for itself! The blood test can help you in living another dimension towards a new beginning in life!

B. Leviticus 17:11 - *For the life of the flesh is in the blood: and I have given it to you upon the alter to make an atonement for your souls: for it is the blood that maketh an atonement for the soul.*

The #7 in the spiritual realm, represents COMPLETION!

Genesis 2:2-3 - *And on the seventh day God ended his work which he had made; and he rested on the seventh day from all his work which he had made. And God blessed the seventh day, and sanctified it: because that in it he had rested from all his work which God created and made.*

VICTORIOUS LIVING THROUGH CHRIST IS THE GOAL!!!!!!!

CHAPTER 8

BREAKING THE STIGMA OF
MENTAL HEALTH DISORDERS

Living with a loved one who suffers with a mental health disorder affects the entire family. You must learn to adapt within the capacity of having a complete change of lifestyle. I've learned to utilize some tools to assist me in coping with my loved one's situation. I've learned to be visual with the mindset of transparency by leaving a word of encouragement that leads to constant prayer. We pray for restoration of the mind, body, and soul and call for complete healing! The process to live a productive and self-sufficient life can be challenging, but don't ever give up on them. Position yourself to be accountable and determine to complete all your own research concerning the information that doctors present regarding their condition. There are programs available to help assist you in coping with any concerns you might have. There are additional professional programs and resources with doctors, counselors and therapists in position to help cope and assist with housing for others suffering with any dysfunctional disorder.

You can research helpful professional options through the National Alliance on Mental Illness (NAMI) or the National Suicide Prevention Lifeline at 1-800-273-8255. These programs offer resources that will help you make life-changing decisions to accommodate your loved one's situation and get them moving towards living a healthier and productive lifestyle!

Having a great support team and system are key factors in receiving healing and strength while helping your loved one. Securing resources, professional advice and professional help are critical while you're going through the trials and tribulations. It's important as you journey towards total healing and maintaining and exceeding expectations for the entire family.

You must have the tenacity, determination and strength to

assist your loved one with guidance to make proper decisions. Get *you* some help as you seek help for them. Ask questions and don't give Satan any credit! I bring this to your awareness because the devil wants to use these strongholds to destroy you and your family. Learn to recognize evil forces in every situation! Continue to stand strong in being an advocate to help break the stigma for those suffering with any mental illnesses.

Let's help spread a positive message to create a change and strive towards transparency as we motivate and educate others who stigmatize your loved one just because they don't look like what they are going through! My brokenness is not the end of my story because I give God all the glory! Whatever the will of God is, you must learn to adjust and press your way through the process.

My son had to appear in court as he was wrongfully beaten by the cops a second time in his life on Christmas Eve 2018. Officers did not understand his mental health disorder. Of course, I initiated my own investigation to find out the truth. As we waited to go before the judge, others were also waiting in the hallway. My son walks and paces the floor quite a bit due to his energy level. I'm equipped to handle it; however, others are not. I don't bother him. I just allow him space to do so.

We arrived early before anyone else. Finally, others began to arrive. I'm sitting and my son was already pacing the long hallway. No one knew he was my son. I observed everyone that arrived, even the officials of the courts (a mother's guard). As they stared (and some began to sigh loudly), I was thinking, "As long as he's not bothering anybody, nobody better not bother him." He was simply walking back and forth! It can be annoying, but it is what it is! This young lady, about 23-24 years old, was so afraid of him that she asked me if she could sit beside me. I said sure and scooted over but there was plenty of additional seating available. I had already observed her staring at my son. She said to me, "Oh, he's scaring me." I said, "Who's scaring you?" She replied, "That guy who keeps walking the floor." I said, "Why is he scaring you? He's not bothering anyone. He's just walking." She said, "I know, but he's creepy to me."

With a very soft voice, I said to her, "I assure you that young man will not harm a fly. He's dealing with a mental health disorder called schizophrenia. He's actually more cautious of you than anything."

Her eyes began to gaze at me as I then began to tell her that he's my son and I purposely observe our surroundings and the people within my range. I also explained that we were in court to clear his record due to the beating he suffered from police officers who also didn't understand him. I smiled at her and cautioned her not to judge others because you never know what a person is dealing with. We both smiled. I told her that God placed her beside me to allow me to explain that situation to her. She felt safe sitting next to me.

I guess I have that motherly love connection of protection over my life. The young lady apologized and thanked me for explaining that to her. I thanked her for receiving the explanation. I informed her that I understood her and that I saw she was already nervous about appearing in court for herself and needed a shield of protection. God used me to shield my son as well as this young lady. GOD IS SO AMAZING!

My experience was part of my spiritual growth, which caused me to grow closer to the Lord and recognize the divine blessings occurring right before my eyes... the remarkable and amazing grace through Christ.

Thank you, Lord, for my trials and tribulations because without them, there would be no growth!

Proverbs 3:5-6 says, *"Trust in the LORD with all thine heart; and lean not unto thine own understanding. In all thy ways acknowledge him, and he shall direct thy paths."*

LORAINE TRAMMELLL

CHAPTER 9

POWERFUL FAITH OVER DEMONIC
FORCES & MENTAL HEALTH DISORDERS

Statistics show that about 1 in 4 Americans suffer with a mental health disorder. Some mental health disorders are the cause of extreme demonic attacks when it comes to self-destruction, destruction towards others or being mixed up in some criminal activity. Among the disorders are schizophrenia, depression; bipolar; Alzheimer; bulimia; suicide; alcohol and drug addictions. The diagnoses from medical doctors are called a chemical imbalance to the brain. These are titles that are considered mental health disorders. The devil attempts to apply many evil plots with strong forces against these titles, by trying to cause disturbance towards the state of your mindset! There are so many young adults dealing with mental illnesses throughout this nation. Sometimes, I feel like this is a war zone of wickedness in high places. Ephesians 6:16 says, *"Above all, taking the shield of faith, wherewith ye shall be able to quench all the fiery darts of the wicked."*

I did not realize that depression was considered a mental health disorder. I was in total denial prior to the research. I thank God that I recognized my situation at an early stage. Once I identified and experienced that something was wrong, I had to accept the fact that my normal activity was interrupted. I was acting in an unusual manner, such as not wanting to communicate with others, always wanting to sit in the dark, avoiding lighted areas, and feeling an additional weight on me as if I was carrying bricks! These were early signs detected, especially due to this not being within my normal character.

You should immediately seek help from mental health professionals, whether it is a counselor or therapist. Most importantly, pray for the covering of God over yourself! You can defeat evil forces attempting to attack your mind with prayer, praise and worshiping the Lord. You cannot fight this battle alone. You will need Jesus!

Attending church allowed me to begin removing scales from my eyes. It gave me a clearer vision of what God was doing with my spiritual growth. I learned to see beyond my flesh and expand my way of thinking. I am now able to operate under the Holy Spirit for his direction in my life. Principalities are throughout the universe! While I press towards my destiny at a higher dimension with Christ, obstacle after obstacle seem to be approaching. Yet, I know I must face the challenges that try to prevent me from being who and doing what God has for me. Sometimes, I feel as though evil forces are attacking from every angle. I remain faithful. Don't be afraid to utilize your spiritual gifts and strengths that God has equipped you with! Isaiah 53:5 says, *"But he was wounded for our transgressions, he was bruised for our iniquities: the chastisement of our peace was upon him: and with his stripes we are healed."*

Recognizing your own self-destruction and self-distress are two ways to detect that something is wrong with you. Evaluate yourself. Do not allow yourself to be overwhelmed with strong emotional stress which wants to take you out. You must remain in prayer.

Having a relationship with Jesus will help you in dealing when you encounter strong forces and attacks that seemingly appear out of nowhere. Anything unusual or out of the ordinary is a red flag that you need to start paying closer attention to who's around you and what's going on around you. But also take that hard, long look in the mirror and see how you are creating the negative changes and experiences. Utilize your trust and faith in God! I believe in praising my way through my trials and tribulations that pop up on this journey called life.

I pray for restoration of the mind, body, and soul of anyone dealing with any afflictions of these titles.

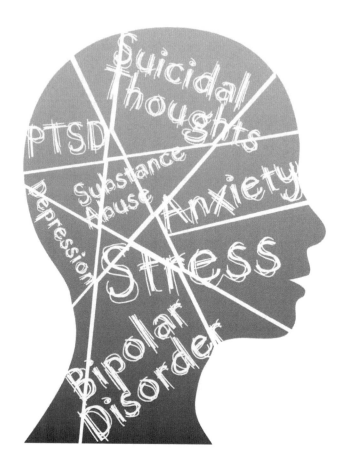

I bind and rebuke any forces of these titles of mental health disorders that are attempting to destroy others. I decree and declare victory over every mental health disorder.

CHAPTER 10

GOD CAN TURN THINGS AROUND

I was in a situation with my older son during one of his schizophrenia episodes. One Saturday afternoon, as I prepared for a family gathering, I wanted my sons to have a moment alone for some brotherly bonding. My younger son moved into his new home and I decided to spend time with him as well that day. I picked up my older son first and then my younger son from work so I could have family time with my two young men. As we traveled to see my younger son's new home, we pulled over to a gas station so my older son could use the restroom. He was having one of his episodes (that's what I call it when he's acting abnormal). So, we had to stop. We all exited the vehicle to allow him his time. My younger son and I approached the counter to pay for items. As we both left the store, we went to the car and waited for his brother. We had no idea he had already left the store. We waited and waited until I returned to the store, had the store manager check the restroom and my son wasn't there. I asked the clerk if he had any more exits or if he saw my son. He said no. He allowed me to check the entire store. My son was nowhere to be found. It was such a crazy moment. We never found him in the store. It was like he just disappeared.

My younger son became extremely upset. We got back into the car to search for him. We had no idea where he could have gone. The area was very small with only a grocery store across the street and a restaurant. We drove several times to see if he was walking. I couldn't give up. I was in constant prayer the entire time. After 20-25 minutes of searching, my son appears out of nowhere. I spotted him near the grocery store entrance. What a relief that came over me. All I could say was, "Lord, I sure do thank you!" I began to glorify God right there in the car because praise is what I do! This is what I call a divine miracle. Only God can handle situations such as this!

He was just wandering in Conyers, Ga., with nowhere to go. I had to convince him to get back into the car, which was a task because he thought that we left him. He finally got into the car after his brother intervened and really influenced him. By this time, the younger son, who was still upset, felt that his brother wanted more attention. I tried to explain that it was more complicated than that and that his brother's situation was very serious. They are so close and it's difficult for my younger son to see his brother with this condition.

It seemed like it all happened instantly, and it was even hard for me as I began as a parent to recognize certain behavioral circumstances. Now that it's here, I must deal with it.

We never made it to my younger son's new home. The episode was too intense on all of us. We made a U-turn! I began to question my son about why he didn't wait by the car once he left the store. He said when he did not see us, he thought that we left him. I never saw him leave and neither did his brother. Everything happened so quickly. He just vanished. All I could do was cry. I was emotionally drained. I had to do a video on my cell phone to encourage myself.

Oh, my goodness! I was feeling some kind of way and I needed the Lord to move on the inside of me. I needed a word of encouragement. I needed to feel a move from God right away. I was instantly granted a spiritual calmness within my soul. My sons were silent the entire trip back to their drop off destination. I had to pray over my family because there was a force of evil trying to destroy us. No devil! Not today, you won't! Thus, said the Lord, my test and trials are ordained through Christ.

I must remain visible to my obstacles and continue to trust

in God, as he directs my path! Some principalities seem overwhelming in your mind, but you must yield and turn it over to God to handle.

Ephesians 1:19-20 says, *"And what is the exceeding greatness of his power to us-ward who believe, according to the working of his mighty power. Which he wrought in Christ, when he raised him from the dead, and set him at his own right hand in the heavenly places."*

CHAPTER 11

PRAYER STILL WORKS

We are living in the days called the Millennium, year 2020. There is so much devastation occurring across this nation! The United States has a president in office who conducts himself like a person with a mental disorder... in my opinion. His actions and decisions in leading the United States are out of control, radical and unhealthy for human beings. The black race is a walking/living target to be shot and killed by police officers for no reason and there is no justification to defend many cases! This is evident by what my family experienced when my son was the victim of police brutality. I never pressed charges because we were more concerned about my son recovering as he was fighting for his life in the ICU in a Tennessee hospital.

My constitutional rights were challenged due to the attack occurring in a different state. To fight the case without complication, I needed to be a resident of that state. I was outside of my boundary, meaning the compliance rules and regulations for an attorney had to be bonded in both states. It was too costly and the search for that type of attorney was a huge task. I had to remain focused on my son's wellbeing and health. Prayer still works!

I am extremely grateful to God for allowing me to complete my second book, despite all the brokenness and obstacles that I've encountered along this journey called life. My prayer and hopes are to help others. If God did it for me, God can do it for you. I continue to ask God to utilize my testimony to nourish, strengthen and save others' soul, and to allow the manifestation of divine intervention to overflow throughout the nation!

It is possible to achieve your goals while spreading the gospel at the same time. When you have a calling on your life through Christ, you must be willing to allow God to use you so you can pursue the work and the will of God for your life. Satan's strategies are filled with trickery and intimidation to stop you from having control over your purpose and your destiny. But prayer still works! Continue pressing your way through every principality that you may experience!

Be visual and aware of wicked forces attempting to destroy you and your character. Make wise decisions on all matters or activities. Never lose sight of what God is showing you or revealing to you. Build a strong relationship with Christ! Redeem yourself! Know that God will never leave you nor forsake you. Learn to recognize that you have the POWER and AUTHORITY through Christ to overcome any obstacle. You are chosen by Christ to make a difference on this journey called life. God is still in the miracle working business and he is performing miracles right before our eyes.

I am yet holding onto my FAITH and pressing my way towards the manifestation of victorious living through Christ! James 2:14 says, *"What doth it profit, my brethren, though a man say he hath faith, and have not works? Can faith save him?"*

I've grown spiritually and I'm now able to recognize my purpose through Christ. I'm able to observe the fight within myself, which makes me a spiritual warrior on the battlefield, with POWER and AUTHORITY granted through the spiritual realm of CHRIST! Through intercessory prayer, I have higher expectations for my life as well as for my children, family members and others. PRAYER STILL WORKS!

- I will remain my course!
- I will remain faithful!
- I will remain vigilant and wise!

God will protect me just as he did Daniel in the lion's den!

Daniel 6:22 – *"My God hath sent his angel, and hath shut the lions' mouths, that they have not hurt me…"*

God will keep me and my family, just as he did Shadrach, Meshach and Abednego in the fiery furnace.

Daniel 3:25 – *"He answered and said, Lo, I see four men loose, walking in the midst of the fire, and they have no hurt: and the form of the fourth is like the Son of God."*

- I will continue to trust God in directing my path!
- I will remain assured that God will fight the battle of wickedness in high places and principalities for me!

As evil forces attempt to slither and lurk, I will keep on my armor of God, stand strong, and fight a good fight to gain VICTORY through Jesus Christ!

I WILL CONTINUE TO HAVE POWERFUL FAITH WHILE CONQUERNG PRINCIPALITIES and RECOGNIZING the POWERS OF GOD!

2 Timothy 4:7 – *"I have fought a good fight, I have finished my course, I have kept the faith…"*

ABOUT THE AUTHOR

Loraine Trammell is a woman of faith and integrity. Born and raised in Atlanta, she has worked for Primerica Financial Services for more than 30 years. Loraine is an advocate and motivational speaker for the mentally challenged, who deal with depression, schizophrenia and ADHD. She is the proud mother of three adult children, David Simpson III, Shane Simpson, and Lorriel' Simpson, and the proud NANAH of two beautiful grandchildren, Londyn and Logan. Loraine is also an actress and full-figured print model with TLA Agency representing self-confidence. In her spare time, she enjoys traveling, modeling, photography, serving in church and spending time with family.